THE SHADOW AT DEADWICK HOUSE

Written by Sana Rasoul
Illustrated by Dan Whisker

hachette
LEARNING

ISBN: 9781036001193

Text © Sana Rasoul
Design, illustrations and layout © 2025 Hodder & Stoughton Limited
First published in 2025 by Hachette Learning,
An Hachette UK Company
Carmelite House, 50 Victoria Embankment, London EC4Y 0DZ

www.HachetteLearning.com
The authorised representative in the EEA is Hachette Ireland, 8 Castlecourt Centre, Dublin 15, D15 XTP3, Ireland (email: info@hbgi.ie)

Impression number 10 9 8 7 6 5 4 3 2 1
Year 2029 2028 2027 2026 2025

Author: Sana Rasoul
Illustrator: Dan Whisker/The Bright Agency
Series Editor: Catherine Coe
Educational Consultant: Pauline Allen
Page layout: Rocket Design (East Anglia) Ltd

With thanks to the schools that took part in the development of *Reading Planet Cosmos*, including: Ancaster CE Primary School, Ancaster; Downsway Primary School, Reading; Ferry Lane Primary School, London; Foxborough Primary School, Slough; Griffin Park Primary School, Blackburn; St Barnabas CE First & Middle School, Pershore; Tranmoor Primary School, Doncaster; and Wilton CE Primary School, Wilton.

The Publishers would like to thank the following for permission to reproduce copyright material. Design: © tutti frutti/stock.adobe.com; © frilled dragon/stock.adobe.com; © Pavlo Vakhrushev/stock.adobe.com.

All rights reserved. Apart from any use permitted under UK copyright law, no part of this publication may be reproduced or transmitted in any form or by any means, electronic or mechanical, including photocopying and recording, or held within any information storage and retrieval system, without permission in writing from the publisher or under licence from the Copyright Licensing Agency Limited. Further details of such licences (for reprographic reproduction) may be obtained from the Copyright Licensing Agency Limited, www.cla.co.uk

A catalogue record for this title is available from the British Library.

Printed in the UK

Hachette UK's policy is to use papers that are natural, renewable and recyclable products and made from wood grown in sustainable forests and other controlled sources. The logging and manufacturing processes are expected to conform to the environmental regulations of the country of origin.

To order please visit www.HachetteLearning.com or contact Customer Service at education@hachette.co.uk / +44 (0)1235 827827

Contents

1 Deadwick House 4

2 Out of Bounds 16

3 Shadow 25

4 The Power of Light 38

5 A Farewell 48

1

Deadwick House

Kae was having the worst possible morning. His mum had dragged him out of bed and hurried him into the car.

"Eat that," she ordered, shoving an apple in his hand.

"I'm not hungry." Kae rubbed the lingering sleep from his eyes. "Why do I have to stay with Uncle Adam for the whole of half-term?"

"We've already spoken about this," said Mum. "I need to fly out for work and your dad is away too. There's no one to look after you except your uncle."

Kae sunk back in his seat as they drove down the motorway on a gloomy October morning. Uncle Adam lived in a small town called Cemetery Grove. Kae had heard all sorts of rumours about it from the kids at school. The houses were said to be very big or very small, with no in-between, and they all had unusual sounding names instead of just house numbers.

"What is Uncle Adam's house called again?" Kae asked.

"Deadwick House," Mum replied.

"Deadwick House …" Kae repeated to himself. An unwelcome shiver ran down his spine.

He'd never been to his uncle's house before.

"Is it creepy and old? Does he have any games? Is there a TV in his house? What am I going to do for the whole week?" He turned to his mum, pleading with his eyes, but it was no use.

"Listen to me, Kae. Remember what I told you about Uncle Adam? He likes the quiet, so try to keep your noise level down whilst you're there."

Kae sulked for the rest of the journey. *This is so unfair*, he thought to himself. He should be spending the week playing video games and finishing off the stash of sweets he'd hidden under his bed, not being bounced from one home to another like a tennis ball.

Kae looked out of the window and sighed; everything around him was grey. The road, the ghostly sky and even the light patter of rain. The further they drove, the greyer and angrier the clouds appeared. Kae sympathised because he was angry too. Both times Kae had met Uncle Adam, he'd been quiet and withdrawn. He reminded Kae of a zombie and not the fun kind either.

"We're here," his mum announced as a rusty gate ahead of them screeched in his ears. That was when Kae laid eyes on the house for the very first time.

"Woah!" He drew in a big breath, not quite believing what he was seeing.

Deadwick House stood in-between drooping trees long abandoned, left to grow wild. The windows were small and square and most of them were boarded up with wooden planks, but even Kae could see that once upon a time the house had been something special.

Kae felt an icy sensation on the back of his neck as soon as he stepped out of the car. The driveway was covered with broken branches and decaying leaves, the colour of rotting oranges. He could hear the echo of his footsteps as they crushed down on the leaves, the noise bouncing off the old bricks of the house and straight into his eardrums.

"Does Uncle Adam live alone?" Kae asked.

"Yes," Mum replied.

"It's very big for one person. Is he rich?" Kae cheered up at the thought — maybe if he befriended his uncle, he'd give him any games console he wanted.

"No, he's not. This house has been in our family for a long time and it clearly needs a lot of work, but your uncle won't let us touch it." His mum shook her head. "Now let's go and say hi."

Kae climbed up the chipped wooden steps, which groaned under the weight of his feet.

He reached for the brass knocker, banging on the front door three times. After a few minutes had passed without a sound, Kae heard the creak of footsteps coming from inside the house. The door slowly opened.

"Hello!" said Kae's mum, opening her arms out affectionately, but Uncle Adam stood in the doorway, as rigid as a pole.

"Oh right, sorry. I f-forgot," his mum stammered. "No touching."

Uncle Adam stared at Kae.

"Kae, say hi to your uncle." Mum gave him a little push.

"Hi," Kae squeaked.

His uncle certainly wasn't rich because rich people didn't have holes in their jumpers and socks like Uncle Adam did. He was tall like Kae's mum and had the same dark eyes, but his shoulders were slumped and his expression was gloomy.

"Come in," Uncle Adam said, although it may as well have been a growl as far as Kae was concerned. From the look on his uncle's face, Kae couldn't help but think that Uncle Adam wasn't very happy to see him. He hadn't thought about it the other way round before. It didn't feel good.

When the door closed behind them, Kae and his mum were plunged into a glum darkness. The furniture was dark, heavy and old-fashioned, as though the house had got stuck in a time machine. The yellow wallpaper was the worst, reminding Kae of his grandad's feet, cracked and peeling at the edges. Uncle Adam walked ahead of them in complete silence.

"Why are all the windows covered in paint?" Kae whispered to his mum.

"Shh! Don't ask your uncle those questions!" Mum said nervously.

"Why not? What's the big deal?"

"He gets very grouchy when you ask him about the house."

This stinks, Kae thought. The house stunk, too, of damp and mould. It became clear to him that Uncle Adam hardly cleaned the place. Kae followed his uncle and mum along the dimly lit corridor into an even darker room, which had only one small sofa and a wooden chair. By now, Kae was sure his uncle was allergic to light, *and* mirrors. Every mirror and window he had passed was splashed with black paint.

Kae grimaced. Something strange was going on at Deadwick House.

"Would you like a cup of tea, or coffee?" Uncle Adam offered. "Mind you, I don't have any of that fancy stuff."

"Oh no, thanks, I'd better be going," Kae's mum quickly replied. "The traffic will pick up soon."

"You're already going?" Kae glared at his mum.

"I'm sorry, darling, but I'm already running late for my flight. Your dad will pick you up on Saturday. Be good, okay?" She kissed him on the cheek and made for the door, waving with a guilty look in her eyes.

Kae turned to his uncle, unsure of what to say or do.

"I'll show you to your room," said Uncle Adam slowly. "Follow me." He led Kae up the spiral staircase. The metal felt cold against Kae's hand.

"How many floors are there?" Kae asked as they climbed up.

Uncle Adam stopped abruptly and snapped his head in Kae's direction, his eyes flashing with something Kae couldn't quite read. It made his stomach jump, like when his mum drove over a speed bump without realising.

"Your room is on the first floor – the second floor is out of bounds."

"Why? What's up there?" Kae immediately wanted to check it out – to explore. As an only child, he was used to amusing himself.

"Storage," his uncle said dismissively. "I don't want to catch you up there under any circumstance, do you understand?" Though there was a harshness to Uncle Adam's voice, when Kae looked at him more closely, he was surprised by how tired and soft his uncle's eyes were.

"I tend to be in my study until the evening so you can entertain yourself out in the garden," Uncle Adam went on. "Kids shouldn't be indoors. It's not healthy."

Kae wanted to tell his uncle that he didn't look so healthy himself. His cheeks were sunken and his black eyes had no shine.

Kae decided it was best to say nothing and just nod along.

"Why are all the windows covered in paint?" he said instead, unable to stop himself asking the question. He noticed how the house seemed to grow darker and colder the higher up he climbed.

"It's cheaper than buying curtains," his uncle replied from over his shoulder.

Why were the mirrors splashed with paint too though? Kae would ask his uncle when he was in a better mood — if that ever happened.

"This is your room." Uncle Adam opened the door to a large room, with a bed three times the size of Kae's bed at home. There wasn't much else in there besides a carved wooden desk, a wardrobe and a bulky chair made of cheap plastic that looked so uncomfortable, Kae couldn't imagine anyone ever sitting on it.

He kicked off his shoes and sat at the edge of the bed. He was always complaining about how tiny his bedroom was, but he wasn't sure he liked big rooms either. Small bedrooms were cosier, and felt safer somehow.

This room was cold — so cold he could feel the icy air sliding through the neck of his T-shirt. The windows in here were splashed with paint too, making Kae feel like he was stuck in a dungeon with a grumpy old dragon.

"There's a lamp there if you need it." His uncle pointed to the bedside table. "I've left you a sandwich in the fridge for lunch. I'll be in my study, so try not to disturb me and don't make too much noise whilst you're at it."

Uncle Adam had a lot of rules.

2

Out of Bounds

Disturbing his uncle was the last thing Kae wanted to do, so he went down to the kitchen to scoff down the bland cheese sandwich before heading outside. At least it would be much lighter out there.

Kae followed the overgrown path into the belly of the garden. It was bigger than he'd expected and to his left was a narrow path that led him directly to a small pond. Kae tried to spot a fish – or a toad – but after staring at the muddy water for five minutes, he got bored and gave up.

He took his time walking back to the centre of the garden, plucking a cherry from one of the trees. It burst with flavour inside his mouth, sweet and tangy at the same time. Kae passed more fruit trees and some large rose bushes before he noticed the small shed tucked behind two towering oak trees. Curious, he drew closer to the shed. It was locked, so he went round to the side and brushed a spider's web from the window so that he could peer inside.

The shed was empty apart from a few rusty garden tools. Kae sighed, but then he heard a rustling movement just behind the shed where the neighbour's fence was. Cautiously, Kae drew closer. He was tall enough to peer over the fence. A girl with bright chestnut-coloured hair looked up at him. She wore blue dungarees that matched her eyes and a jacket that was far too big for her.

"Hi," Kae said.

"Hello." She smiled at him. "I'm Jasmine."

"I'm Kae."

"Do you live in Deadwick House?" Jasmine asked.

"I'm staying with my uncle for the half-term but I'm bored already. There's no TV or anything," Kae complained.

"Dad has a new computer and he's let me download a few games on it. Do you want to play tomorrow?"

"Sure!" Kae nodded enthusiastically.

"I've got to go but come round to mine tomorrow." Jasmine waved as she ran into the house.

"Back already?" Uncle Adam was by the door when Kae came in. He wondered if his uncle had been watching him the entire time, but that was not possible. There were no clear windows to look out from.

"There was nothing to do," Kae said. "But I met a girl called Jasmine. She's—"

"I know who she is," Uncle Adam snapped.

"Can I play with her tomorrow? She's got games on her dad's computer."

"Hmph," Uncle Adam said, which Kae took to mean yes. "You kids have no imagination these days. It's all that technology."

"I need to rest my head for a bit, but I shouldn't be longer than half an hour," Uncle Adam announced, sounding weary.

Kae fell silent.

"If you insist on staying inside, don't go poking your nose where it doesn't belong," he warned, but Kae knew that would be hard. He couldn't help it. He was an explorer after all.

Kae waited ten minutes before pressing his ear against his uncle's door.

He heard a deep grumble. His uncle was fast asleep and snoring – now was his chance to explore the house. He only had twenty minutes left, so he had to be quick.

Careful not to make a sound, he made his way up to the second floor. Kae shuddered from the cold.

He tried to open the door but it was locked.

Kae reasoned that if Uncle Adam used the locked room for storage, the key must be in the house. Knowing his uncle, he'd either keep it close to him or somewhere he knew no one else would dare go. Kae checked his watch and saw he had fifteen minutes left. He crept down the stairs as quietly as a mouse and started trying doors. It wasn't long before he found the study but Kae's confidence dipped when he saw how many books there were.

What if Uncle Adam had hidden the key inside one of them? He'd never find it in time. He decided to tackle the desk first, opening and closing the drawers. There was no sign of a key.

Kae picked up books from the shelves at random, ruffling through the pages. He made sure to put them back properly so his uncle wouldn't notice. There were only ten minutes left now and he was about to give up on the whole thing – until he saw his uncle's jacket draped over a hook on the door.

He ran towards it, digging into the pockets until he felt the sharp edge of something. With his heart thumping, Kae pulled out a gold key with specks of black paint around the edges. Even though Kae was sweating, the key felt like a pocket of ice-cold air in his hand. This had to be the key to the locked room, didn't it? There was only one way to find out.

Rushing upstairs, Kae put the key in the lock and heard a resounding click. He smiled to himself. Bravely, he entered the room and instantly felt as though his lungs were being squeezed tight. The shivering cold was what he imagined the Arctic Ocean to feel like.

After his eyes had adjusted to the darkness, Kae gasped …

Uncle Adam's obsession with paint was clear to see in here – everything was covered in thick black paint. The walls, the windows, even the floor. Every crack of light that could have possibly entered had been suffocated by the darkness.

Kae spotted a light switch, but when he clicked it he realised the bulbs had all been smashed, the sharp pieces of glass left on the floor. Uncle Adam had lied about this being a storage room — apart from a small black box in the middle of the floor, there was not much else. Tentatively, Kae walked towards the box but froze when he heard a voice.

"Hello, my name is Shadow. What is yours?" It sounded like a young boy whispering.

Fear gripped Kae's throat and refused to let go. He wanted to run in panic, but the explorer in him had other ideas. Squinting through the darkness, Kae tried to find the source of the voice.

"Who's there?" Kae said, his voice cracking.

"I'm Shadow. What is your name?" the voice repeated. That was when Kae realised the voice was coming from *inside* the box. Carefully, he bent down and reached for it with both hands. It felt like ice.

"H-How did you get in there?" Kae stuttered. "What are you?"

Before whatever was in that box could respond, Kae heard footsteps below him, followed by a loud bang.

Uncle Adam was up!

Shadow

Panicking, Kae quickly placed the box back on the floor where he'd found it.

"I have to go, but I'll come back again tomorrow," Kae said, although he felt silly for talking to a box.

There was a small silence, in which Kae thought he had imagined the whole thing, but then he heard a low drawn-out cry coming from the box.

"Kae! Where are you?" Uncle Adam's voice boomed from the floor below, making him jump on the spot. Afraid his uncle would catch him doing something he wasn't supposed to, Kae closed and locked the door behind him and ran down the stairs into his room. He barely had time to process what had happened when his door flew open. Uncle Adam poked his head inside.

"You're here," he said, relief in his voice. "I thought you were outside; I've been looking for you in the garden."

"I have a stomach-ache so I was just resting for a bit."

Kae didn't want to lie, but until he figured out what was going on, he couldn't tell the truth either.

"Very well. I'm just heading to the study."

"What? Now?" Kae asked, panicking that he'd find the key gone from his jacket. "Erm, actually, Uncle Adam, I'm a little hungry. Can you make me something?"

Uncle Adam huffed and his shoulders slumped.

"Another sandwich okay?" Uncle Adam took the bait like Kae had hoped.

"Thank you," Kae said, managing a smile, but Uncle Adam only stared at him before he glared around the room as if searching for something. He shook his head, muttered something under his breath and shuffled out.

Kae waited at the bottom of the stairs just to make sure Uncle Adam was really in the kitchen before placing the key back in the study where he had found it. He spent the rest of the evening looking for clues as to what Uncle Adam was hiding, but it was impossible with Uncle Adam keeping a watchful eye on him. Kae was sure that his uncle was keeping something from him, and he wanted to know what.

The next morning, when the sun had barely revealed its face, Kae got out of bed and stood outside his uncle's room. He pressed his ear against the door and listened.

Uncle Adam was snoring, so Kae ran to the study and took the key from Uncle Adam's jacket once again. He glanced around him nervously, tightened his fist around the key and left the room.

An eerie silence filled Deadwick House, broken only by Kae's heavy breathing and the creak of floorboards as he climbed the stairs up to the second floor. He unlocked the door and walked into the frosty room; the box was still there. He picked it up and brought it close to his face.

"Hello?" he whispered. "Shadow? Are you there?"

Kae waited, his hands shaking and his breath getting louder. He didn't quite know what he was waiting for but he continued regardless, licking the sweat off his upper lip.

"You came back," Shadow said.

Kae gave a startled jump.

"Don't be afraid of me," the voice told him.

Kae edged closer, a million questions racing through his mind.

"Are you really inside the box?" he finally said, swallowing the lump in his throat.

"Yes, please help me," Shadow pleaded. "Put me near the light to free me."

Kae looked around him hesitantly, too afraid to move. What exactly was going to come out of that box?

"Please!" Shadow sounded desperate.

Kae couldn't see how he was going to get any light in the room, so he picked up the box and walked out into the corridor. A sliver of yellow light beamed from the window in the far corner of the corridor, where the paint had peeled off.

With shaking hands, Kae held the box close to the window, bathing it in a warm glow. Sucking in his breath, he watched the air filling with thick grey smoke as the top of the box opened.

Out of it emerged a boy-shaped silhouette that appeared by Kae's side just like a shadow would. It had no face so Kae couldn't tell what it was thinking. He wanted to know everything about Shadow right away, but a small noise from downstairs broke Kae's startled trance.

"I have to go," Kae whispered urgently.

"I go where you go. I'm now *your* shadow."

Kae didn't have time to ask what Shadow was talking about. He placed the box in the centre of the room, locked the door and ran downstairs to put the key back where he'd found it. He thought about going back to his room, but decided it was safer to be out in the garden. He didn't want his uncle eavesdropping on him and Shadow.

"Thank you for freeing me," Shadow said, sliding onto the grass to face him, shifting his form so that it looked exactly like Kae. Well, his height and shape at least. Kae took a step back; his legs felt like jelly.

"Are you a ghost?" Kae said, unable to hide the crack in his voice.

"No, I'm simply a shadow."

"But shadows don't talk ..."

"Some of us do," Shadow said, a little too quickly. "The special kind."

A flicker of regret washed over Kae. The feeling came on suddenly, just like the cold draft that circled him. He shrugged it off and turned back to Shadow.

"How did you end up in the box?"

"Your uncle—" Shadow paused and cleared his throat, "Adam trapped me in the box when he no longer wanted me to be his shadow."

"Uncle Adam?" Kae gasped, feeling terrible at the thought of being locked away in the darkness. Why would his uncle be so cruel?

"Why didn't he want you to be his shadow anymore?" Kae asked.

"He didn't like shadows; he vowed to get rid of all of them. Adam never liked having anyone close to him."

Kae couldn't believe what he was hearing. He knew Uncle Adam was a loner and that he was strange, but he never imagined him hurting anyone.

"How did he trap you in the box?"

"He weakened me by starving me of all light," Shadow said, a sadness to his voice that made Kae sad too.

"That's why it's so dark in the house …" Kae thought out loud. "Won't Uncle Adam notice you've gone from the box?"

"No, he never opened it again, out of fear. When he sees me, he will just think I'm a normal shadow. Only you can hear me."

Looking at Shadow, Kae couldn't help but wonder what other secrets Uncle Adam was hiding from him ...

"Kae! Come inside and have some breakfast," Uncle Adam's voice travelled from the house to his ear. Kae looked at Shadow in a panic.

"It'll be all right," Shadow soothed. "Act like I am not there."

"Kae! I won't ask again," Uncle Adam growled.

Kae took a deep breath and walked back into the house. His uncle was sitting at the breakfast table in the kitchen sipping on a steaming mug of coffee. When he saw Kae, he pushed a plate of runny eggs and burnt toast towards him.

"Thank you," Kae muttered. Even though his stomach was growling, Kae couldn't bring himself to swallow the food in front of him.

"You're not eating," Uncle Adam remarked, a quizzical look on his face.

"I'm not very hungry. Can I go round to Jasmine's house instead?"

Uncle Adam cleared the plate and looked at him.

"As long as you don't bring her back here," Uncle Adam barked.

"Who is Jasmine?" Shadow asked as soon as they stepped foot out of the house.

"She lives next door – we said we'd play together today. I'm hoping we might be friends."

"I tried to be Adam's friend," Shadow said, "but he got tired of me. Instead of freeing me, he left me to rot in that box." Kae couldn't tell if Shadow was upset or angry or both, but there was a stinging bitterness to his words. Rightly so, thought Kae – he'd feel the same if someone locked him up.

Kae couldn't find the words to comfort Shadow. The adrenaline rush that had got him up at an early hour now dipped, tiredness catching up with him. He yawned loudly as they reached Jasmine's house.

It was shaped like a castle tower and had many windows, reminding Kae of church windows. The house was cheerful and inviting – the total opposite of Uncle Adam's.

Kae knocked on the door and waited. Seconds later, it was opened by a smiling Jasmine. She was still in her pyjamas and had what looked like an apple pie in one hand.

"Oh hi, Kae! I didn't think you'd come so early," Jasmine said, taking a big bite of the pie, apple sauce dripping down her white top.

The smell of cinnamon filled Kae's nostrils but still he couldn't muster an appetite. *Strange*, he thought – the smell of anything sweet usually stirred his stomach in a good way.

"Hey, yeah, sorry. I can come back later if you're busy?" Kae said.

"No, it's okay – you can be my excuse not to do the million chores Dad wants me to finish. Come in." She ushered him inside. Kae, along with Shadow, followed her to a room with a massive TV, a computer and a games console.

They sat on the floor in front of the TV, legs tucked underneath them as Jasmine swallowed the last chunk of pie. Shadow was quiet, and for a moment Kae even forgot he was there.

"Do you want some pie? We've got plenty left."

"I just had breakfast, thank you," Kae said. "Does your house have a scary name too? I've heard lots about Cemetery Grove – apparently tons of creepy stuff happens here."

"It's called Wormwood House," Jasmine said.

"There aren't worms here, are there?" Kae commented, looking around him nervously.

Jasmine thought about his question before answering.

"I haven't seen any myself, but my sister told me she saw a snake swimming in the bathtub once."

"A snake?"

"I don't believe her of course — Gilly's always saying wild things. Like the other day, she said she saw a tiny mermaid in the lake behind our garden."

Kae belly-laughed at that.

"She's four so I can't get annoyed about it." Jasmine grinned from ear to ear and Kae wanted to smile back, but he couldn't shake off the wave of drowsiness washing over him.

"Ready for a game?" Jasmine said.

Kae shook himself to snap out of his drowsiness.

"Yes! Get ready to lose!"

"As if! **No** one has ever beaten me yet," Jasmine said, a smug smile on her face.

A few hours later, Kae and Jasmine finally put down their controllers. Kae lay flat on the floor and stared up at the white ceiling. There were no cracks or mould like the ceiling in Uncle Adam's house, Kae thought. Lucky Jasmine.

"Do you want to go to the garden and play football?" Jasmine asked.

"Yeah, sure," Kae said, but he made no effort to move.

"Are you okay?" Jasmine sat up and looked at him. "You look very pale."

"It's been a strange morning ..." he said.

"Strange how?" Jasmine asked, moving closer to him.

Kae quickly got to his feet. He'd almost got carried away and told Jasmine about Shadow but he had to protect Shadow's secret until he decided what he was going to do.

"I should get back. Thanks for letting me play," he said weakly.

"Rematch tomorrow?" Jasmine asked. She'd beaten Kae the whole time and normally his ego would be bruised, but he was too tired to care.

Kae nodded and left Wormwood House with Shadow.

That evening, the house was yet again submerged in silence. Kae was in his bedroom when Shadow turned to him.

"Would you like me to tell you a story?" he said.

"What kind of story?" Kae replied.

"Any kind you like."

"Scary stories are always fun," Kae said.

Shadow began telling story after story, and the more he spoke the more tired Kae felt. His eyes were like two heavy rocks, and he struggled to keep them open. In the end Shadow's voice sent Kae into a dreamy haze filled with nightmares. Kae tossed and turned, sweat drenched his clothes, and once or twice he was convinced Shadow himself was standing above his bed.

Watching him in the dead of night.

4

The Power of Light

Kae woke up the next morning and immediately knew something was very wrong. His muscles ached, his thoughts were fuzzy and his eyelids refused to stay open. Shadow on the other hand seemed full of energy. It was as if, by some kind of magic, Shadow had grown stronger overnight whilst Kae had become weaker. He sat up slowly and watched as Shadow stirred in the corner – there was something different about Shadow's movements today.

"Let's head outside," Shadow pleaded. "I've been cooped up in the dark too long."

"I'm not feeling well," Kae said. "Maybe later."

"It will make you feel better, getting some fresh air," Shadow insisted, much to Kae's annoyance. He liked having Shadow around, sure, but he was becoming more and more demanding of Kae's time.

"Fine," Kae gave in.

He shuffled to the bathroom whilst Shadow hovered outside the door. Kae took his time getting changed, relishing the time alone even if it was just for a brief moment. Maybe, just maybe, he understood why Uncle Adam wanted Shadow out of the way. No, Kae wasn't thinking straight. His thoughts were too muddled to make any sense.

Finally, Kae came out of the bathroom and headed downstairs for a glass of water. The inside of his mouth felt like the Sahara Desert, parched and sucked dry of any moisture.

"We'll go out only for a bit, okay?" Kae told Shadow at the bottom of the stairs.

"Who are you talking to?" came a voice from the kitchen doorway. Kae turned; his uncle was looking at him, his eyes like those of a hawk. They narrowed as he glowered at Kae, sending a chilling wave down his back.

"Oh ... n-n-o ... no one," Kae said quietly. "I mean, I was speaking to myself. I do that sometimes." Kae tried to laugh it off but it hurt his throat.

"Are you heading out?" Uncle Adam said.

"Yes, you said I should spend lots of time outside," Kae reminded him.

"I suppose I did, but eat something first, will you? I can't have your mother thinking I haven't fed you," his uncle grumbled as he walked to the study.

Kae went out into the garden and sat on the grass, hoping he'd feel better in time for his rematch with Jasmine.

"Adam has changed," Shadow broke the silence.

"What do you mean by that?"

"He wasn't so ... reclusive then."

"Reclusive? What does that mean?"

"It means he doesn't spend time with people."

Kae raised an eyebrow, a memory nagging at the back of his head.

"I thought you said Uncle Adam didn't like having people near him when you were his shadow and that's why he didn't want you around?" Kae asked.

"What? Oh ... yes ... I-I mean he was a little nicer before."

The garden began to spin in front of Kae's eyes, the trees, leaves and grass blending into one giant green blur. He rubbed his eyes, blinked, and breathed a sigh of relief when his focus returned. What was going on with him? He shook his head and turned to Shadow.

"You haven't told me anything about special talking shadows like you. How many are there? How come some shadows speak and others can't?" Kae didn't know why he was asking Shadow all these questions but something inside pushed him to – a disturbing feeling he couldn't shake off.

"Oh that ... it's a heavy story, I'll tell you another time," Shadow dismissed him.

Kae turned his face away. He didn't believe Shadow. Shadow loved talking, even about scary things, so why was he so reluctant to talk about his past now?

Rubbing the dirt off his trousers, Kae stood up and headed straight for the fence that backed onto Jasmine's garden.

"Where are you going?" Shadow asked. "To Jasmine's again?"

"Yes," Kae said.

"Stay out here for a bit longer," Shadow told him.

Kae froze on the spot.

Shadow had sounded different just then. Like a proper grown-up, with a stern warning to his tone that Kae didn't like.

"Don't you like Jasmine?" Kae said.

"It's nicer out here – there's more light."

"I'm sorry, but I said I'd go," Kae told Shadow.

Shadow didn't say anything, which made Kae feel on edge. On top of that, his temple suddenly pulsed with pain.

"I-I think something's wrong with me," Kae said quietly, but if Shadow heard him, he didn't say anything.

Kae climbed over the fence with the dwindling energy he had. It took all of his effort to get across. Just as he was about to go round to the front of Wormwood House and knock on the door, Jasmine appeared from behind a bush with a spade in her hand.

"Kae! You scared me!" Jasmine cried out. "I can't play just yet; Dad wants me to plant these flowers before the sun disappears!"

"I really need to talk to you," Kae whispered, glancing at Shadow from the corner of his eye.

Kae shifted his weight from one foot to another in an attempt to control his growing alarm. Ever since he'd opened the box with Shadow in it, he'd not been feeling like his usual self.

"You don't look well – are you okay?" Jasmine put down the spade.

Kae stared at Shadow. It was now or never. He brought his mouth close to Jasmine's ear and whispered.

"I opened a box that Uncle Adam had hidden in the house and now I'm starting to think I shouldn't have."

His confession felt like a weight off his shoulders. Like he could breathe again.

"What was in the box?" Jasmine asked loudly.

Kae put a finger to his lips and stared at Shadow. Jasmine followed his gaze and looked at Shadow with a confused look on her face. Shadow was angry, very angry. Kae could feel the anger coming off him, or it – Kae wasn't sure anymore what to call Shadow. The angrier Shadow became, the more disorientated Kae felt. His feet wobbled underneath him; Jasmine grabbed him by the arm before he could fall.

"Tell me everything," Jasmine said, a look of determination on her face, and so Kae did. He told her about the second floor, how he'd found the key to the room with the box in and how smoke had come out of it, morphing into a shadow, *his* shadow. When Kae finished whispering all of this to Jasmine, he heard Shadow next to him hissing like a wild animal.

Kae took a few steps back, but Shadow followed him.

"What's happening?" Jasmine yelled.

Kae couldn't explain without arousing Shadow's anger again.

"You do believe me, don't you?" he asked.

"I do," Jasmine said. "But how did your uncle trap him the first time round?" she asked quietly, with one fearful eye on Shadow.

"I think he did it by making the house dark and putting Shadow in a box. Light must give Shadow energy."

"Then you have to do the same ..." Jasmine said.

"How, when he's attached to me? It won't be easy putting him back in the box. I'd have to go in with him ..."

"Take away his light until he gets too weak to stay as your shadow. Then you can put him back in the box."

"But that means ..." Kae stared at Jasmine in disbelief.

"You have to lock yourself away in the dark," Jasmine said, and the very thought made Kae shrivel up into a tight ball.

A gust of wind blew him to the side. Kae staggered backwards but managed to remain upright.

"I think Shadow knows what we're planning," Kae whispered.

A small sound came out of Jasmine.

She put her hand on his shoulder and squeezed it.

"You can do this! It won't take long to drain him of strength, right?" Jasmine asked, but truth was, Kae didn't have the answer to that. He wished he could turn back time to before he'd gone up to the second floor. It was out of bounds – why hadn't he listened to Uncle Adam?

"What will I tell my uncle?" Kae said, panicked.

"Tell him you're sick and you don't want him to catch anything. You can't leave your room until Shadow separates from you! I'll come check in on you the day after tomorrow – I won't be back until then as we're staying at my nan's tonight."

Kae was scared, but he didn't want to admit it to Jasmine. His body flushed with heat but he felt cold and shivery at the same time. Zipping up his coat and pulling the hood over his head, Kae braced himself for what was to come.

"I should go now," he said and Jasmine hugged him goodbye.

"Stay strong," she told him. "Don't let that thing take any more of your light."

Spurred on by her words, Kae walked quickly, conscious that every second was now precious in a way it wasn't before. He had already exposed Shadow to too much light, and he now needed to suffocate it with darkness. He didn't dare to think what would happen otherwise.

"I know what you want to do — you're just like Adam," Shadow growled at him but Kae didn't respond. He was too paralysed by fear. If only he could tell his uncle about what was happening to him. He'd know exactly what to do — he'd done it before. But Kae knew that wasn't an option, because he'd be in big trouble for not listening to him in the first place.

A Farewell

"Uncle Adam?" Kae shouted as soon as he was back inside the house. "Uncle Adam!" he tried again.

"My goodness, what is it? Why are you yelling?" He came into the hallway scratching his beard and looming over Kae with a scowl on his face.

"I'm not feeling too good. I think I'll stay in my room for the rest of the day."

"What's wrong with you?"

"My tummy hurts and it might be contagious so I'll stay upstairs until I feel better."

"You kids are always catching things. Go upstairs and I'll heat up some soup."

"Just leave it outside my door and I'll eat it when I can," Kae said, not wanting Uncle Adam to barge in on him. He turned and hurried up the stairs before he could say anything else. Shadow had been quiet this entire time. No more hissing, or growling. No more scornful words.

For Kae, the silence was much more terrifying than all the noise.

Kae closed the door behind him and got to work. First, he took out the bulb from the lamp near his bedside table.

His eyes swept through the room, searching for other sources of light. The paint on both windows was cracked at the corners. Kae dug into his suitcase and pulled out a couple of his old T-shirts. In the bathroom, he searched through the cabinet until he found a roll of thick transparent sticking tape, which he used to stick his clothes over the window.

Satisfied that no light, however weak, could enter the room, Kae wrapped himself up in a blanket and closed his eyes. He expected Shadow to put up a fight, to protest, to try to trick Kae into stopping what he was doing, but Shadow wasn't talking to Kae anymore.

What exactly was Shadow planning?

"Kae?" his uncle said from behind the door. "I'm leaving the soup out here."

"Thanks, I'm just getting into my pyjamas. I'll eat it later." Kae coughed for effect, although he did genuinely feel unwell. It was obvious that Shadow wasn't just feeding off light, he was also draining Kae of his energy.

When night came, Kae began to feel worse, and Shadow's eerie presence meant Kae couldn't let himself fall asleep. He had to stay awake, just in case. He didn't know anything about Shadow, which meant he didn't know what he was truly capable of with enough power.

Kae listened to the pounding beat of his heart, remembering Jasmine's words right before she hugged him, using them as comfort. He'd see her soon; he only had to get through one more day, and who knows, Shadow might be gone by then. Kae allowed himself to stay optimistic until it was no longer possible to hold off sleep. It came for him, just as Shadow had.

The next day, Kae's hopes of getting Shadow into the box seemed like an impossible feat. Kae was feeling weaker, and deprived of natural light, Shadow was even greedier for Kae's energy. Kae could feel it. Kae sat on the edge of the bed as the birds cawed outside, yearning for the open air. He wanted to be in his bedroom back home, full of colour and games and sweets and all his other comforts.

A knock on the door roused him from his daydream. The sound echoed in his ears. Kae cleared his itchy throat and looked around the room in a frenzied panic. He grabbed the thin sheet from the bed and wrapped it around him, trembling from the cold.

"Don't come in, Uncle Adam. I'm really very unwell," Kae said.

"You need to eat. Open the door."

Kae knew he couldn't hold off his uncle for the whole day, so he rushed to the door and opened it just enough to push his head out.

"Oh!" Uncle Adam's eyes grew large with worry. "You look awful."

Concerned words were not what Kae wanted to hear right now. It only made it harder to keep his uncle away from the truth.

"I'll stay in here again today, Uncle Adam."

"Yes, that's wise, but you have to eat something, otherwise you won't get better and it'll mean a trip to the doctor." He picked up the tray from the floor and gave it to Kae. On a cracked plate were two pieces of dry toast, a measly amount of butter spread on top of them, and orange juice with pips in it. Feebly, Kae took the tray from Uncle Adam, who was watching him closely.

"Thanks," Kae said before shutting the door behind him again.

Kae turned back to the room and forced himself to eat the toast, but it was like biting into chunks of rock. Tasteless and solid. The orange pips stuck to his teeth. The one thing that kept him going was the thought of seeing Jasmine tomorrow.

Shadow was on the wall today, like a dark painting that refused to wash away. Kae knew, as surely as he knew his own name, that Shadow was enjoying all of this. He couldn't prove it of course, but he felt it, and sometimes feelings were all you had to go on.

Why wasn't Shadow weakening? What was Kae doing wrong? Kae buried his head in his lap and vowed not to give up. He couldn't let Shadow win, even if it meant another night locked away by himself.

When night did finally arrive, Kae was restless. He'd hoped to see signs of Shadow turning back into smoke, but none came. Instead, he battled with sleep the whole night.

By the following morning, the uncertainty of his plan made him uneasy. Pacing up and down the room, Kae tried to steady his racing heart. Shadow mimicked his movements. His outline appeared more solid than it had last night – another reminder that his plan wasn't working.

"What do you want from me?" Kae yelled. It was the first time either of them had uttered a word to each other since he'd locked himself up in the room.

Shadow didn't say anything.

"Tell me!" Kae demanded, but Shadow only laughed.

A commotion at the door pulled Kae's attention away from Shadow.

"I can check in on him – you don't have to come with me. Really, it's fine."

Jasmine! She was here, like she'd promised.

"I'm going in, step aside," Uncle Adam spoke, his voice clear and firm. Kae turned to Shadow, then to the door.

It was too late to try to cover his tracks – the bulb lay on the floor and his T-shirts were hanging over the window with a criss-cross of thick tape.

The door burst open, and Uncle Adam and Jasmine stepped into the musty room with horrified looks on their faces. Uncle Adam took one look at the room, pausing at the windows, before his eyes settled on Kae.

"My word, what have you done, boy?" he gasped. It was the first time Kae had seen something other than annoyance or worry in his uncle's eyes.

Uncle Adam was scared.

"I'm sorry," mouthed Jasmine.

"Kae? What is the meaning of this?" his uncle said, inspecting the windows closer. When Kae didn't say anything, Uncle Adam looked down at the floor, at his own shadow and at Jasmine's. Then, his eyes slowly moved to the wall where Shadow was hanging.

He wheezed, a growing realisation on his face.

It was Kae's turn to apologise now.

"I'm sorry, I didn't know ... I opened the box ... I've tried to keep it in the dark, but it won't go away."

Jasmine rushed forward, a drawstring bag hanging from

her shoulder, but Uncle Adam grabbed her by the arm to stop her getting close to Kae.

"What do we do now?" Jasmine turned to Uncle Adam.

"You say he hasn't weakened?" Uncle Adam asked.

"I think I gave him too much light when I took him out of the box," Kae explained.

"My old friend, Adam," Shadow's coarse voice hit Kae in the stomach.

"Did you hear that?" Kae said, edging backwards.

"Hear what?" Jasmine said.

"It spoke," Kae whispered. "Be careful, Uncle Adam."

Kae's uncle hesitated before taking a few steps closer to Shadow.

"Finally, we can be reunited," Shadow cackled, "just like old times."

Kae was beginning to feel lighter, as though something heavy was being lifted off his shoulders. He looked up and saw Shadow reach for his uncle.

"Uncle Adam! He's trying to be your shadow again!"

In a swift move, Kae's uncle reached for Shadow's leg, tugging him off the wall, but Shadow simply exploded into a puff of grey smoke. Uncle Adam fell backwards as the smoke circled him. Kae and Jasmine rushed forward and pulled Uncle Adam to his feet and away from the encroaching smoke.

"Give me your bag," Kae told Jasmine. "Quick!"

"What are you going to do with it?" she asked.

"We need to put Shadow in here before he attaches himself to Uncle Adam. It's our only chance," Kae said, turning to find the grey smoke moving towards his uncle.

Kae and Jasmine each held one side of the bag and used it as a net to capture the smoke, but it swerved past them in a fury that knocked both of them to the ground.

"Take me, I'm here!" Uncle Adam yelled, goading Shadow towards him instead. The smoke darted straight for Kae's uncle, like a perfectly aimed arrow. "NOW!" Uncle Adam yelled.

Kae and Jasmine lunged forward with the bag, forcing it over Shadow, but small puffs of smoke poured out of the open gaps at the top of it.

Uncle Adam raced forward and held the bag steady whilst Kae reached for the drawstring, fastening it at the top together as tightly as he could. After a few moments, the bag stopped shaking and everything went quiet.

It was Jasmine who smiled first.

Kae collapsed on the bed. He could finally breathe again.

"Give it here – I'll put it back in the box." His uncle held out his hand, but Kae didn't move.

"No, Uncle Adam. If you keep him here, you'll always have to make sure the house is dark and gloomy."

"I have no choice; it's been like this for many years now. I'm used to it."

"I know what to do ..." Jasmine said quietly.

Kae and Uncle Adam turned around at the same time.

"We'll bury him far away from here. It means you can have light again in the house," Jasmine told Uncle Adam.

"That sounds like a good plan, don't you think, Uncle Adam?" Kae said.

He stood in front of Kae, nodding, his eyes shining as if he was on the verge of tears.

"I'm sorry I didn't listen to you," Kae said meekly.

Uncle Adam opened his mouth and closed it again, like a fish gasping for air.

"It worked out in the end." Kae's uncle smiled, and his whole face changed in that moment. The three of them walked down the stairs together.

"You should go home now before your dad gets worried. I'll make sure Shadow is buried far away from here," Uncle Adam told Jasmine. "I don't know why I didn't think of that before."

"Can I come over later?" Jasmine asked with a slight hesitation in her voice.

Kae looked at his uncle with anticipation.

"You're welcome here anytime." Uncle Adam gave them both a big smile and that made Kae smile too.

Kae felt a pang of sadness when he heard the rumble of a car drive through the gates on his final day at Uncle Adam's house. The last few days had gone quickly – a blur of hanging out with Jasmine and helping Uncle Adam to strip the paint off all the windows and mirrors.

Kae carried his suitcase down to the hallway. "It looks much nicer in here now there's plenty of light."

Uncle Adam nodded.

"You're absolutely right. I should get some new furniture too."

"And Wi-Fi," Kae laughed.

"Cheeky boy!"

"Can I come visit again soon?" Kae said as he heard a bang at the door. He wanted to make sure his uncle was okay – plus he knew he'd miss him, and Jasmine.

"I'm counting on it," Uncle Adam replied.

"I'm just going to say goodbye to Jasmine quickly." Kae ran into the garden and climbed over the fence. Jasmine was waiting for him.

"Are you leaving now?" she said.

"Yes, my dad is here, but I'm going to come back very soon, okay?"

"You had better," Jasmine said, "we're friends forever now."

"Friends forever," Kae said.

In the car, Kae's dad looked apologetic. "I know you weren't happy at us leaving you there, and your mum and I are sorry," he said as soon as they drove off.

"I wasn't happy at first, but actually, I had a great time! I want to come back again, but this time, can I stay longer, Dad?"

Kae's dad looked at him in surprise, a smile forming on his lips.

"You've changed your tune, haven't you? I don't see why not."

Kae smiled to himself and turned to the window. He thought he'd noticed a wisp of smoke in the corner of his eye, but when he rolled down the window, all he could see was the clear, bright sky.

Now answer the questions ...

1 Where did Uncle Adam live?

2 Kae grimaced on page 11. What does 'grimaced' mean?

3 Why was Kae so happy to meet Jasmine?

4 What did you think would happen when Kae unlocked the room on the second floor?

5 The author describes the regret that Kae felt on page 30: 'The feeling came on suddenly, just like the cold draft that circled him.' How do the words used add to the meaning?

6 Why did Kae start to feel weaker and weaker during the story?

7 How did Kae, Jasmine and Uncle Adam capture Shadow?

8 Have you read any other stories about spooky houses? What happened in them?